The Knowing Heart

Love Poetry by Nancy Hull

HOUNSLOW

The Knowing Heart
Love Poetry by Nancy Hull

Publisher: Anthony Hawke
Cover/Interior Photography: by Nancy Hull
Designer: Gerard Williams
Compositor: Accurate Typesetting Limited
Printer: Gagné Printing Ltd.

Canadian Cataloguing in Publication Data
Hull, Nancy, 1947 —
    The knowing heart
ISBN 0-88882-135-2
I. Title
PS8565.U55K5 1990 C811'.54 C90-095341-1
PR9199.3.H85K5 1990

Hounslow Press
A Division of Anthony R. Hawke Limited
124 Parkview Avenue
Willowdale, Ontario, Canada M2N 3Y5

Printed and bound in Canada

Knowing truth.

Acknowledging "N" and his inspirations.

Thanks also to friends, colleagues, and mother for
encouragement.

Special appreciation for the technical staff
who worked so carefully on the production of this book.

CONTENTS

FOR
THOSE
IN LOVE

ABOVE THE MIST

see that tree

      somewhere between
      yesterdays and
      tomorrows

      it surges forth

      infallibly
      directing its
      sable-green
      chorus

      above the mist

      it sings of love
      to the listening
      sky

SEA QUESTIONS

like a magical shore
you evoke
the nurture
of my
kisses

over and over

each time
something
of my sea
is absorbed
into your
tawny satin
sands

oblivious to
broken-hearted
shells
strewn along
the back of
your shore

shells
vacuous
now filling
with dust

the tip of
a stretched wave
almost touches
them

and a pool
of questions
takes itself
to the sea

will I too
be betrayed

an abandoned shell

or will I be
of meaning

the One
integral with
your life

the sea
recedes

contemplates
the depth of
blue-green
echoes

looks again
to your
persuasive
shore

and returns

with trust

NEXT MOVE

some
trap hearts
in a game of cards
guessing outguessing
to nowhere

night
veils their
stealthy return to
silt-smothered feigned
habitats

they
long for
iridescent fields
and flowers of
mutual growth

    but know not
    the next move

SCENE STUDY
IN THE DOORWAY

i.
anticipation
opens my
door

ii.
your reassurances
sweep into my
arms

iii.
if the door closes
what will live
on the
inside

and on the
outside
?

INSPIRATION

an
empty canvas
you were there
existing in a bland
corner of the world

unfurled when you
came to me

       our colours
       mingled and
       swirled easily

       into radiant ribbons
       of dew-fringed
       blossoms

       breathing
       continuous
       affection

this adoration of you
brought fresh summers
and growth

new life
and strength
within yourself and
within our blending

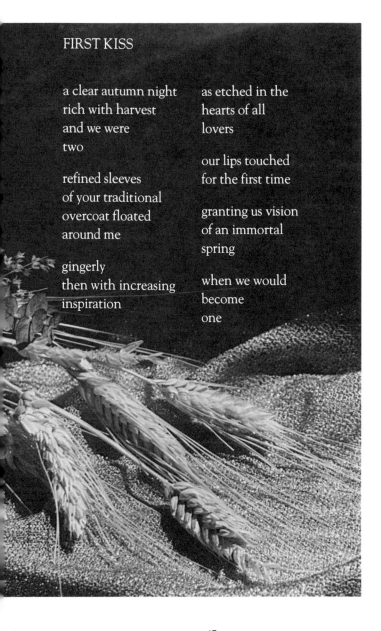

FIRST KISS

a clear autumn night
rich with harvest
and we were
two

refined sleeves
of your traditional
overcoat floated
around me

gingerly
then with increasing
inspiration

as etched in the
hearts of all
lovers

our lips touched
for the first time

granting us vision
of an immortal
spring

when we would
become
one

17

CRYSTAL WISHES

I saw
your wishes

restless within those
well-defined facets
of the crystal chalice

as
your
sunbeams
moonbeams
and delicate
dreams

were beginning
to flow out of
transparent
tableaux

and into us

DISCLOSURE

love-words
can be used the way
they were meant to be
sturdy forests of shelter and
nourishment to make each other strong

love-words
however can be used as
treacherous nets hurled upon us
by those preying on our vulnerability

love-words
can feed either side

SUPPRESS

eyes barren
you veer

sudden fear
steals you
unable to respond

    I seek to understand
    but your signs
    crumple
    my text

    and the next
    love-lights
    are sent
    unwillingly

    to the underground

TIME FOR DISCUSSION

details decisions
revisions

we convene
a murmur of words

you sit directly
across from me
knowing that last night
had become enshrined
in a dream

> *a purple sky*
> *dusted with diamonds*
> *we drift hand in hand*

pragmatically
you say we must
focus plan
schedule

moonlight moves
across your hands
drawing feathery caresses

tea is poured into
elegant cups
and our fingers slide
around the handles

delicate fragrance and
reflections of blue petals
curl around us

you proceed with
geometric words
we should we ought
not

uncertain eyes
intercept

tendrils of amber light
have slipped through
open windows

with quiet gentleness
your hand enfolds mine

wordless
we drift into

the welcoming twilight

A SONG FOR YOU

with
just a glance

you elicit my inner song

    shimmering
    pure
    sure
    in its direction

serene sounds
this consecrated
gift

to enhance
not by chance

a song
for you

YOU ASK WHY

along the pathway of
a champagne rose
we pause
        as you ask why

you are skimming my face
with such enticing and
caring eyes
that I am held
in a trance
        and you ask why

your fingertips slowly
caress the contours of
my lips and when I
respond with a soft kiss
        you ask why

you draw me close to you
and I let my head take in
the security
of your cozy chest
        and still you ask why

you sense the
glimmering filaments of
an invisible bond
enwrapping us together
        and of course you ask why

only when you hush
your pedantic probe
you begin to see
that the heart
does not always
rationalize

it just knows

UNSPOKEN
PROCLAMATION

today
we wanted to say it
to each other
but words eluded us

today
we spoke silently
through the passion
of our mirrored gaze

today
sparkly constellations
proclaimed what we
craved and deserved:

I do love you

TRADITION

lovers love
to give-receive
teddy bears

cuddly
crush-proofed
symbols of
caring

SILVER VASE: I

given awkwardly
it had attempted
to conceal
residual shyness
in you

the
silver vase

recalls that
ephemeral
moment
when a
first gift
seemed to move
of its own accord
from your
nervous hands
to mine

tenderly
it was placed
on the lace-draped
dresser where
it would rest
regally

awaiting

SILVER VASE II.

reflections
in smooth
silvery surfaces

shiny rivulets

our romance
flowing
creating
through the
years

ALMOST TOO LATE

coerced by
steely-eyed
time pieces

you were a
flurry of
jumbled fingers
determined
to jam
scrunched toes
into an
inside-out
sock

my compassion
saw your life

and came to
rescue

THE VOW

my
whole
being
is the
vow

eternally
faithful

it surpasses
paper promises

BATHROBES

I
like
your
bathrobe
cuddling
the hanger on
back of the door

shared space in
this safe harbour

with mine

PHOTOGRAPH

Fixed in thought
your image
is stationed
at the
bedside table

undaunted

guardian
of the
night

OASIS

underneath
the narrow tedium
and sunless papers
of a frantic day

we form an
oasis

luxuriating
in melodic lines
that intertwine

we are
a sensual sonata

replenishing
each other
with warm
realness

LOOK TO SUNSETS

when
others try to
compress you

into trendy diets
ill-fitting shoes or
status to be objectified

look to sunsets

savour their magnific
imperfections

skies
marbled
uncontrived
with shapeless
clouds of
aureate colours
interweaving
like love

this artistry
creates perfection
unable to be
duplicated or
sealed into a jar

for the uniqueness
of each sunset
and you

look to sunsets

and be reminded of
my unconditional love

STARS

snowflakes
are tiny stars
nesting
softly
in your
eyelashes

my instinctive
thoughts
to kiss them

are cautioned

stars
sometimes
fall
to trailing
tears

POTENTIAL PERIL

never
let it fester

impermeable silence

a volcanic wall
capable of
   suffocating hearts
     from within

unresolved
torrential pain
   and devastation
     for both of us

never
let it happen

DOUBLE MESSAGE

inDecisive
fast fOrward rewind
rUnning
love-Blind towards
overLoaded
mEssage mess

WINTER EVE

a silent room
devoid of touch
watching
gray snowdrops
sliding down the
frail window pane

miscues
misunderstandings

why

why does this happen
to those who
love
?

SOMETIMES

just to

hold
each other

and know strength
of quiet moons and
ancient willow trees

keys for comforting
counsel

sometimes
in this emotional journey

it is all we need

PICNIC

remember
that January

winter winds
were screaming
terrorizing
ice-laden
windows

indoors a
benevolent
beach towel
outstretched
carefully
on the secluded
living room floor

we adorned it

a wicker tray
inundated with
tropical treats and
lavish liquid for two

an alluring universe
encased by arched glow
of sweet jasmine candles

such craziness
some might say

but
a cathedral it was
beckoning continuance
of our shadowy contours

and we
embraced this
affirmation

something
to hold onto

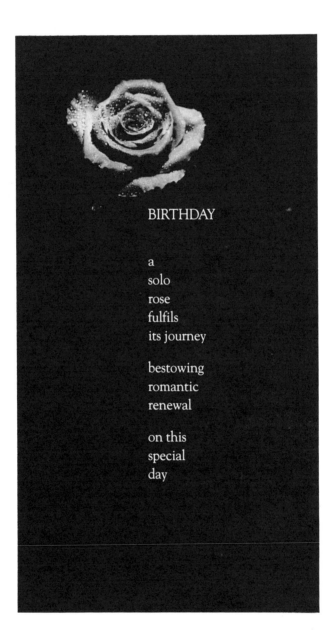

BIRTHDAY

a
solo
rose
fulfils
its journey

bestowing
romantic
renewal

on this
special
day

EMPOWERMENT

yes
there comes a time
when someone something
intervenes the music

and we seem to
slip apart

but it is
seeming and
temporary

for
we shall never
be made
dissonant

we simply merge
into memory of
our expressive
dance

lustrous lyrical
and loving

until the music
is brought back
into focus

yes
to dance again
our timeless rhythms
believing

TRUTH

dawn
  suspends itself
    into an infinite
      moment

discloses
  a lush landscape
    gracing your
      skies

      lucid

      as a blue heron
      reflecting on
      scented silhouettes
      of honeysuckle
      and azaleas

      each fold
        unfolded
          is meticulous

          the more I look
          the surer I am

          this emotion
          is the ultimate

          one can have
          for another

HANDLE WITH CARE

in this darkened sanctuary
my face nuzzles the warmth
of your smooth shoulder

lying here
so near and so far
from you

my hand traces nuances
in the stillness of
your body

searching
wondering where you are

or if
if careful words
could reach through this
insecure time

your eyes close

to verbalize anything
might cause you to
crystallize
shatter into fragments

you breathe effortlessly

and then without a sound
your hand wafts over my wrist

to curve softly
around receptive fingertips

giving light

you dissolve uneasy darkness

THE CALL

on this night

your voice
is the
cloud-covered
moon

barely audible

straining anxiously
through disjointed
telephone waves

stressed

split-second message

you
are on your way

needing the
certainty
of our solid
embrace

to dust away clouds

on this night

AFTER ALL

our touch
passes by
    envious eyes of
    transient tinsel
    and stalements

we hold
silvery secrets
    uncrumbled loving
    still new

    after all
    these
    years

ALWAYS

even
through heavy haze

the knowing
shall guide a seabird
incessantly
to find its way

so too

my heart
shall always open its
luminous path
for you

for us

LETTER FOR THIS MOMENT

dearest

        life may not seem
        to be beautiful
        at times
        confined compelled
        by dutiful walls

        but look beyond

        cherish these
        our beautiful moments
        reverently formed
        into beautiful
        memories

        giving
        living

        perpetually

        in the
        soul

            with love

CODA

my love
you are my only love
worthy of luscious spaces

and so I give to you

      i
      the countryside path
      to hear my whispers
      in the wind

      ii
      where you may drift
      to saffron sunshowers
      of kisses glistening
      with warmth

      iii
      and at your touch
      the velvet blossoms
      always tell you
      I am here

      iv
      here with you
      in a constant moon
      understanding
      dreams and tears

v
and as winter
paints the hours
ivory with
snowswept hillsides

vi
there are patterns
of a note
only you could
really know

but wherever be
the spaces in time
my love

please treasure
in your heart
that I am forever
loving you